ELLIOTT CARTER

RETROUVAILLES

for solo piano

www.boosey.com
www.halleonard.com

HENDON MUSIC

DISTRIBUTED BY

HAL•LEONARD®
CORPORATION
7777 W. BLUEMOUND RD. P.O. BOX 13819 MILWAUKEE, WI 53213

Commissioned for Pierre Boulez,
on the occasion of his 75th birthday, by the Royal Festival Hall

First performed March 26, 2000 by Rolf Hind
at South Bank Center, London

RECORDINGS

Charles Rosen: Bridge Records 9128

Winston Choi: l'empreinte digitale ED13164

Duration: 2 minutes

NOTE BY THE COMPOSER

Retrouvailles for piano, commissioned by the Royal Festival Hall in London, was written to celebrate the 75th birthday of my friend, Pierre Boulez, March 26, 2000. The score returns to the motto

$$B\flat, (o), U, L, E, (z)$$
$$t \quad a$$

used in my *Esprit Rude/Esprit Doux I* (for his 60th birthday) and *Esprit Rude/Esprit Doux II* (for his 70th). Retrouvailles begins by recalling the end of *Esprit Rude/Esprit Doux II* and ends by recalling the opening of *Esprit I*. I hope this work gives some small suggestion of the great admiration I have for this extraordinary musician.

—Elliott Carter

ANMERKUNG DES KOMPONISTEN

Retrouvailles für Klavier, das von der Royal Festival Hall in London in Auftrag gegeben wurde, wurde zur Feier des 75ten Geburtstages meines Freundes Pierre Boulez am 26. März 2000 komponiert. Darin kehrt das Motto immer wieder zu

$$B\flat, (o), U, L, E, (z)$$
$$t \quad a$$

zurück, das ich schon in meiner Komposition *Esprit Rude/Esprit Doux I* (zu seinem 60. Geburtstag) und wiederum in *Esprit Rude/Esprit Doux II* (zu seinem 70. Geburtstag) verwendet habe. *Retrouvailles* beginnt mit einer Wiederholung des Endes von *Esprit Rude/Esprit Doux II*, und endet mit dem Anfang von *Esprit I*. Ich kann nur hoffen, dass in diesem Werk meine große Bewunderung für diesen einmaligen Musikkünstler zu einem gewissen Grad zum Ausdruck kommt.

—Elliott Carter

NOTE DU COMPOSITEUR

Retrouvailles pour piano, commandé par le Royal Festival Hall de Londres, a été écrit pour célébrer la soixante-quinzième anniversaire de mon ami, Pierre Boulez, le 26 mars 2000. La partition retourne au thème

$$B\flat, (o), U, L, E, (z)$$
$$t \quad a$$

Utilisé dans mon *Esprit Rude/Esprit Doux I* (pour son 60ᵉ anniversaire) et *Esprit Rude/Esprit Doux II* (pour son 70ᵉ). *Retrouvailles* commence en évoquant la fin d'*Esprit Rude/Esprit Doux II* et se termine en rappelant l'ouverture d'*Esprit I*. J'espère que cette œuvre donne une petite idée de la grande admiration que je porte à ce musicien extraordinaire.

—Elliott Carter

Pour Pierre en célébration de son soixante-quinzième anniversaire avec souhaits
pour une longue et heureuse vie et avec profonde admiration et amitié affectuese.

RETROUVAILLES

Elliott Carter
(2000)

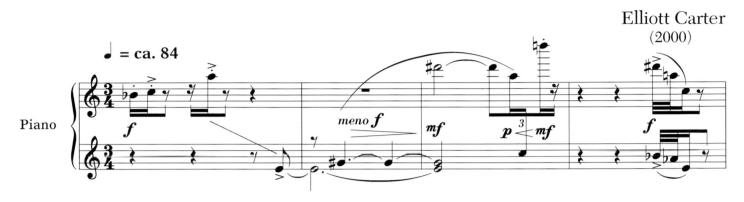

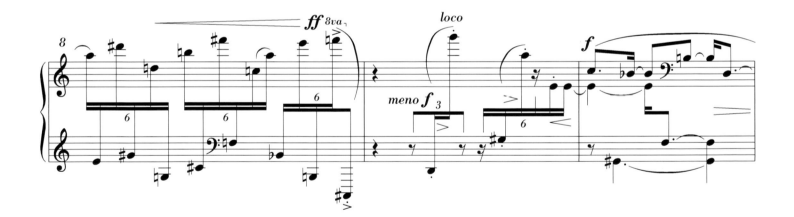

M-051-24625-0

Printed in U.S.A.

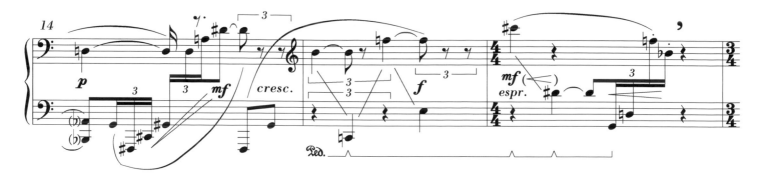

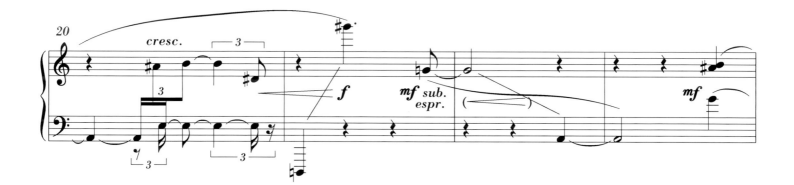

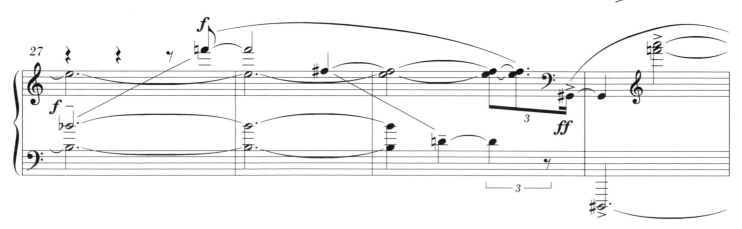

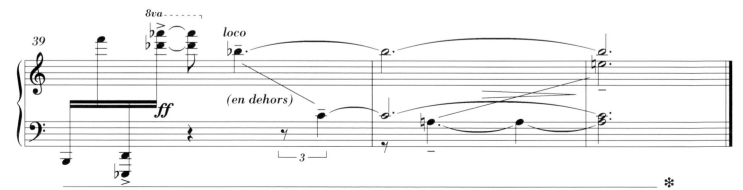